The Art of Loving God

Also available from
Sophia Institute Press
by St. Francis de Sales:

Thy Will Be Done:
Letters to Persons in the World

St. Francis de Sales

The Art of Loving God

Simple Virtues for the Christian Life

SOPHIA INSTITUTE PRESS®
Manchester, New Hampshire

The talks contained in *The Art of Loving God* were published originally in a collection of St. Francis de Sales's conferences delivered to the Visitation nuns, entitled *The Spiritual Conferences*, translated from the French by Abbot Gasquet and Canon Mackey, O.S.B. (London: Burns & Oates, Ltd., Benziger Brothers, 1906). For this 1998 edition, there have been extensive editorial revisions and improvements in the translation.

Printed in the United States of America

Sophia Institute Press®
Box 5284, Manchester, NH 03108
1-800-888-9344

Library of Congress Cataloging-in-Publication Data

Francis de Sales, Saint, 1567-1622.
[Vrays entretiens spirituels. English.]
The art of loving God : simple virtues for the Christian life / St. Francis de Sales.
p. cm.
Originally published as : The spiritual conferences. London : Burns & Oates Ltd., 1906.
Includes bibliographical references.
ISBN 0-918477-42-5 (alk. paper). — 0-918477-43-3 (pbk. : alk. paper)
1. Virtues — Early works to 1800. 2. Spirituality — Catholic Church — History — 17th century. 3. Spiritual life — Catholic authors — Early works to 1800. I. Title.
BX2179.F8V74 1996
241′.4 — dc20 96-8387 CIP

14th printing

Contents

Introduction

Not all of us are called to do great things for the love of God and our neighbor, but we can all do little things each day with greater fidelity and love. Therein lies the essence of St. Francis's teaching in these talks given to the nuns of the Visitation convent in Annecy in the Savoy.

The Visitation was founded in 1610 for widows and unmarried women who wished to live a life of prayer and contemplation withdrawn from the world, but who could not tolerate the harsh austerity of the prominent women's orders of the day, such as the Franciscan Poor Clares and the Carmelites.

In the early years of the Visitation, St. Francis came often to hear the nuns' confessions, offer Mass, and give informal talks on the sort of modest virtues that were to be embodied in the life of the community. Often St. Francis gave these talks out of doors under the trees surrounding the convent, the beauty of the natural setting suggesting many of the charming and homely images he uses to illustrate the points he wants to make. Written down by the nuns as the talks were delivered or shortly afterward, these Spiritual Conferences were copied and widely circulated among Visitation houses, and cherished as precious monuments to their founder's faith, wisdom, and kindly good sense.

Just like the Visitation nuns, many of us in the world cannot, for various reasons, adopt the rigid austerities or heroic self-sacrifice of the great ascetics of the Christian tradition. We, too, must be content with striving for lives of simple virtue and humble service to Christ and His Church. For this reason, we publish those of St. Francis's spiritual conferences that teach us simplicity, humility, generosity, and other such simple virtues for everyday life.

Because this edition of St. Francis's talks to the nuns of the Visitation convent is intended specifically for laypersons, we have generally omitted points that pertain exclusively to convent life and have occasionally adapted St. Francis's wording (such as when he begins a phrase with the address "Sisters") so that the beautiful universality of these virtues will not mistakenly be circumscribed by the context in which St. Francis spoke of them.

Some of the original conferences address more than one virtue. In certain cases, we have divided those conferences into separate chapters, giving each the name of the virtue explained.

The Art of Loving God

1

Have confidence in God's mercy

(from Conference II)

You ask me if a soul sensible of its own misery can go with great confidence to God. I reply that not only can the soul that knows its misery have great confidence in God, but that *unless* it has such knowledge, the soul cannot have true confidence in Him; for it is this true knowledge and confession of our misery that brings us to God.

All of the great saints — Job, David, and the rest — began every prayer with the confession of their own misery and unworthiness. And so it is a very good thing to acknowledge ourselves to be poor, vile, abject, and unworthy to appear in the presence of God.

"Know thyself" — that saying so celebrated among the ancients — may be understood as applying to the knowledge of the greatness and excellence of the soul (so that it may not be debased or profaned by things unworthy of its nobility); but it also may be taken to refer to the knowledge of our unworthiness, imperfection, and misery.

Now, the greater our knowledge of our own misery, the more profound will be our confidence in the goodness and mercy of God, for mercy and misery are so closely connected that the one cannot be exercised without the other. If God had not created man, He would still indeed have been perfect in goodness, but He would not have been actually merciful, since mercy can only be exercised toward the miserable.

You see, then, that the more miserable we know ourselves to be, the more occasion we have to confide in God, since we have nothing in ourselves in which we can trust. The mistrust of ourselves proceeds from the knowledge of our imperfections. It is a very good thing to mistrust ourselves, but how will it help us, unless we cast our whole confidence upon God and wait for His mercy? It is right that our daily faults and infidelities should cause us some shame and embarrassment when we appear before our Lord. We read of great souls like St. Catherine of Siena[1] and St. Teresa,[2] who, when they had fallen into some fault, were overwhelmed with shame.

[1] St. Catherine of Siena (c. 1333-1380), Dominican tertiary and mystic.

[2] St. Teresa of Avila (1515-1582), Spanish Carmelite nun and mystic.

Have confidence in God's mercy

Again, it is reasonable that, having offended God, we draw back a little in humility and from a feeling of embarrassment, for even if we have offended only a friend, we are ashamed to approach him. But it is quite certain that we must not *remain* at a distance, for the virtues of humility, abjection, and shame are intermediate virtues by which the soul must ascend to union with God.

There would be no point in accepting our nothingness and stripping ourselves of self (which is done by acts of self-abasement) if the result of this were not the total surrender of ourselves to God. St. Paul teaches us this when he says, "Strip yourselves of the old man, and put on the new";[3] for we must not remain unclothed, but must clothe ourselves anew with God. The reason for this little withdrawal is only so that we may better press on toward God by an act of love and confidence. We must never allow our shame to be attended with sadness and disquietude. That kind of shame proceeds from self-love, because we are troubled at not being perfect, not so much for the love of God, as for love of ourselves.

[3] Cf. Col. 3:9-10.

Act confidently regardless of your feelings

And even if you do not *feel* such confidence, you must still not fail to make acts of confidence, saying to our Lord, "Although, dear Lord, I have no feeling of confidence in Thee, I know all the same that Thou art my God, that I am wholly Thine, and that I have no hope but in Thy goodness; therefore I abandon myself entirely into Thy hands."

It is always in our power to make these acts; although there may be difficulty, there is never impossibility. It is on these occasions and amid these difficulties that we ought to show fidelity to our Lord. For although we may make these acts without fervor and without satisfaction to ourselves, we must not distress ourselves about that; our Lord loves them better thus.

And do not say that you repeat them indeed but only with your lips; for if the heart did not will it, the lips would not utter a word. Having done this, be at peace, and without dwelling at all upon your trouble, speak to our Lord of other things.

The conclusion of this first point, then, is that it is very good for us to be covered with shame when we know and feel our misery and imperfection; but we must not stop there. Neither must the consciousness of these miseries discourage us; rather it should make us raise our hearts to God by a holy confidence, the foundation of which ought to be in Him and not in ourselves. And this is so inasmuch as we change and He never changes; He is as good and merciful when we are weak and imperfect as when we are strong and perfect. I always say that the throne of God's mercy is our misery; therefore the greater our misery, the greater should be our confidence.

2

Embrace God's will with equanimity

(from Conference II)

You must know that to practice self-abandonment and to forsake ourselves is nothing else but to yield up and surrender our own will so that we may give it to God. For, as I have already said, it would be of no benefit at all to renounce and forsake ourselves, if it were not done to unite ourselves perfectly to the divine Goodness.

It is, then, with that aim only that we must make this act of renunciation, which would otherwise be useless, and would resemble those of the ancient philosophers, who made admirable renunciation of all things and themselves under the vain pretense of devoting themselves to philosophy. Take, for example, Epictetus, a very famous philosopher,[4] who, having been born a slave, was offered his freedom on account of his great wisdom. But he, by the most extreme act of renunciation that there can be, refused to accept his liberty. So he went on voluntarily living in a state of slavery, and in such

[4] Epictetus (c. 50-130 A.D.), Stoic philosopher.

extreme poverty that after his death, nothing was found in his possession but a lamp, which was sold at a very high price because it had belonged to so great a man.

As for us, we should desire to abandon ourselves only in order that we may leave ourselves at the mercy of God's will. Many people say to our Lord, "I give myself wholly to Thee without any reserve"; but very few actually practice this self-abandonment, which is nothing else but the acceptance with perfect equanimity of all the events that befall us, just as they arrive by the order of God's Providence: affliction equally with consolation, sickness with health, poverty with riches, shame with glory, contempt with honor. (I refer to the action of the higher part of the soul, for there is no doubt that the lower part of our soul and our natural inclinations will always tend rather toward honor than contempt, toward wealth than poverty, even though we know that contempt, abjection, and poverty are more pleasing to God than honor and the abundance of riches.)

Obey God's known will and His good pleasure

Now, in order to practice this self-abandonment, we must obey the known will of God, and also the will of

His good pleasure: the one by resignation and the other by indifference. The known will of God includes His commandments, His counsels, His inspirations, and the guidance of our spiritual directors.

God's will of good pleasure concerns events that we cannot foresee. For instance, I do not know if I shall die tomorrow; I come to see that it is the good pleasure of God that I do, and I abandon myself to His good pleasure and die willingly. In the same way, I do not know whether in the coming year all the fruits of the earth will be destroyed by storms and unfavorable weather; if it should be so, or if a pestilence should break out, or whatever may happen, it is quite evident that it is the good pleasure of God, and therefore I conform to it. It may happen that you have no consolation in your spiritual exercises. Now, it is certain that this is the good pleasure of God; therefore you must remain perfectly indifferent between desolation and consolation. You must do the same with regard to all things that may occur to you, including the clothes that are given to you and the food that is offered to you.

I must, moreover, observe that there are matters in which the known will of God must be united to the will of His good pleasure. For instance, suppose I fall sick of a malignant fever. In this event, I see that it is God's good pleasure that I should be quite indifferent as to whether I am ill or well; but the known will of God is that I should call in a doctor and apply all the remedies possible (I do not say the very best remedies, but the common and ordinary ones). God has shown this to us by giving healing power to remedies; Holy Scripture in various places teaches us to do so; and the Church commands it.

Having done this, whether the malady conquers the remedies or the remedies get the better of the malady should be a matter of perfect indifference — so much so that, if sickness and health were put before us, and our Lord were to say to us, "If thou choose health, I will not deprive thee of a single particle of my grace; if thou choose sickness, I shall not in any degree increase that grace, but in the choice of sickness there is a little more of my good pleasure," the soul that has wholly forsaken itself and abandoned itself into the hands of our Lord will undoubtedly choose sickness, solely because it is more pleasing to God. Even though this might mean a whole lifetime spent in bed in constant suffering, the soul would not for anything in the world desire to be in any other condition than this.

Thus the saints in Heaven are so closely united to the will of God, that if there were even a little more of His good pleasure in Hell than in Heaven, they would leave Heaven to go there. This state of self-abandonment comprehends also perfect submission to the good pleasure of God in all temptations, dryness, dullness, aversions, and repugnance that come upon us in the spiritual life, for we see in all these things the good pleasure of God, when they do not happen through our own fault and there is no sin in them.

To summarize, self-renunciation is the virtue of virtues: it is the cream of charity, the odor of humility, the merit, I consider, of patience, and the fruit of perseverance. Great is this virtue, and alone worthy of being practiced by God's most beloved children. "Father," says our dear Savior on the Cross, "into Thy hands I commend my spirit."[5] It is as if He said, "It is true that all is consummated and that I have finished all that Thou gavest me to do; but yet, if it is Thy will that I should still remain on this Cross and suffer more, I am content to do so; into Thy hands I commend my spirit. Thou canst do with me as it pleases Thee." We ought to

[5] Luke 23:46.

do the same on all occasions, whether we suffer or enjoy some consolation, allowing ourselves thus to be guided by the divine will at its good pleasure, without ever permitting ourselves to be preoccupied with our own will.

Trust in Divine Providence

Our Lord loves with a most tender love those who are so happy as to abandon themselves wholly to His fatherly care, letting themselves be governed by His Divine Providence, without any idle speculations as to whether the workings of this Providence will be useful to them to their profit, or painful to their loss. This is because they are well assured that nothing can be sent, nothing permitted by this paternal and most loving Heart, which will not be a source of good and profit to them. All that is required is that they should place all their confidence in Him, and say from their heart, "Into Thy blessed hands I commend my spirit, my soul, my body, and all that I have, to do with them as it shall please Thee."

Never are we reduced to such an extremity that we cannot pour forth before the divine Majesty the perfume of a holy submission to His most holy will, and of a continual promise never willfully to offend Him. Sometimes our Lord wills that the souls chosen for the service of His divine Majesty should content themselves with a firm and unchanging resolution to persevere in following Him amid the disgusts, dryness, repugnance, and asperities of the spiritual life, without consolation, delight, sweetness, or relish, and indeed believing themselves unworthy of such things. They thus follow their divine Savior with the fine point of the spirit, with no other support than that of His divine will, by whose good pleasure it is thus.

Now, you ask me what you should occupy your mind with, once you have entirely given yourself into the hands of God. You have nothing to do but to remain close to our Lord, without troubling yourself about anything, either regarding your body or your soul, for since you have committed yourself to the Providence of God, why do you need to think about what will become of you? Our Lord, to whom you have entirely surrendered yourself, will think of everything for you. (I do not, however, mean to say that we must not think about the things to which we are bound by our respective duties; for it would not be right for anyone, under pretense of having given himself up wholly to God and throwing all his care on Him, to neglect whatever is needful for the duties of his state of life.)

Let our Lord carry your soul

It is quite true that it takes a very great confidence thus to abandon ourselves without any reserve to Divine Providence; but then, when we abandon everything, our Lord takes care of everything and orders everything. On the other hand, if we reserve anything to ourselves, instead of confiding it to Him, He leaves it to us, saying as it were, "You think yourselves wise enough to manage this matter without me; well, I will leave you to do so. You will see how you will succeed."

Mary Magdalene, who had given herself up wholly to the will of our Lord, remained at His feet and listened while He spoke.[6] When He ceased to speak, she also ceased to listen, but still, she never stirred from the place she had taken near Him. So it is with the soul that has surrendered itself; it has nothing else to do but to rest in the arms of our Lord like a child on his mother's breast. When she puts him down to walk, he walks until

[6] Luke 10:39.

she takes him up again, and when she wishes to carry him, he allows her to do so. He neither knows nor thinks where he is going, but allows himself to be carried or led wherever his mother pleases. So the soul that has abandoned itself to God lets itself be carried when it lovingly accepts the will of God's good pleasure in all things that happen, and walks when it carefully does all that the known will of God demands.

You ask me now if it is possible that our will should be so absolutely dead in our Lord, that we no longer know what we wish or what we do not wish. I reply in the first place that, however much we may have renounced ourselves, we always retain our liberty and our free will to such a degree that some desires or volitions stir within us. These, however, are not absolute volitions or complete desires, for as soon as a soul that has abandoned itself to the good pleasure of God perceives within itself any volition, it immediately puts it to death, in order to make the will of God live in its place.

Abandon yourself to God's will even in prayer

You may wonder if a soul, still very imperfect, can with profit to itself remain in prayer before God with that simple attention to His divine presence. I tell you that if God places you there, you can certainly remain there, for it happens not infrequently that our Lord gives this repose and tranquillity to souls that are still striving for perfection.

There are very perfect persons to whom our Lord never gives this sweetness and repose, who do all in the higher region of their souls, and who by the sheer force of the higher reason, make their own will die and God's will live in them. This death is "the death of the cross,"[7] which is much more excellent and generous than that other. It should rather be called a slumber than a death, because a soul that has embarked in the vessel of God's Providence lets itself be carried gently along, like one who, although asleep in a boat on a quiet sea, is all the time making progress. This manner of death, so gentle and so sweet, is given by a free gift, the other by merit.

Rely on God's goodness, not on your feelings

Our confidence in God must be founded on His infinite goodness and on the merits of the Passion and

[7] Phil. 2:8.

death of our Lord Jesus Christ, with this condition on our part: that we should preserve and recognize in ourselves an entire and firm resolution to belong wholly to God, and to abandon ourselves in all things and without any reserve to His Providence. Observe that I do not say that we must *feel* this resolution to belong wholly to God, but only that we must have it and recognize it in ourselves; we must not concern ourselves with what we feel or do not feel, since the greater part of our feelings and satisfactions are only the movements of self-love.

Neither must it be supposed that in all this practice of abandonment and indifference, we shall never have desires contrary to the will of God, or that nature will never shrink with repugnance from the dispositions of His good pleasure, for these will often occur. The virtues of abandonment and indifference reside in the higher region of our soul; the lower region, generally speaking, has nothing to do with them. We must remain at peace, and paying no attention whatever to what that lower nature desires, we must embrace the divine will and unite ourselves to it — whatsoever this may entail. There are very few persons who reach this height of perfect self-renunciation; nevertheless, we must all aim at it, each according to his little measure.

3

Practice humility to increase your generosity

(from Conference V)

Humility is nothing else than the recognition that we are absolute nothingness, and it keeps us constant in this estimation of ourselves.

To understand this better, you must know that there are in us two kinds of good gifts: some that are both in us and of us, and others that are in us but not of us. When I say that we have good gifts that are of us, I do not mean that they do not come from God, and that we receive them from ourselves; for, in truth, of ourselves we have nothing but misery and nothingness. Rather, I mean that they are gifts that God has placed within us in such a manner that they seem to be actually of us. Such gifts are health, riches, learning, and the like.

Now, humility prevents us from glorying in or esteeming ourselves on account of these gifts, which it holds as of no account at all. And it does this with reason, seeing that they are most unstable possessions, they do not render us more pleasing to God, and they are mutable and subject to the caprices of fortune.

Indeed, is there anything less secure than riches, which depend on the weather and seasons; than beauty, which may fade in a moment, and which some little disfigurement on the face suffices to blemish; or than learning, seeing that some little brain trouble can make us forget and lose all that we once knew?

Value the gifts God gives you

It is, then, with great reason that humility takes no account of all these gifts. But the more it makes us humble and abase ourselves through the knowledge of what we are of ourselves and through the small esteem in which it holds all that is in us and of us, so much the more, on the other hand, does humility also make us greatly esteem ourselves on account of the good gifts that are in us but not of us: faith, hope, the love of God (little though it be in us), and a certain capacity that God has given us of being united to Him by grace. And this esteem in which humility holds all these good gifts — namely faith, hope, and charity — is the foundation of generosity of spirit.

Humility believes that it can do nothing, considering its poverty and weakness, if we depend on ourselves.

On the contrary, generosity makes us say with St. Paul, "I can do all things in Him who strengthens me."[8] Humility makes us mistrust ourselves; generosity makes us trust in God.

You see, then, that humility and generosity are so closely united to one another that they never are and never can be separated. There are persons who deceive themselves by a false and foolish humility, which prevents them from looking at the real good that God has implanted in them. In this they are quite wrong, for the gifts that God has bestowed on us ought to be recognized, esteemed, and highly honored, and not placed in the same rank or held in the same low estimation as those that belong to the gifts that are in us and of us.

Not only have true Christians always recognized that these two kinds of gifts must be regarded in different aspects, the one kind as given for our humiliation, the other to glorify the divine Goodness that bestowed them; the philosophers, too, have done the same. Their maxim "Know thyself" must be understood as referring not only to the knowledge of our vileness and misery, but also to that of the excellence and dignity of our

[8] Phil. 4:13.

souls, which are capable of being united to Divinity by His infinite goodness, because He has implanted in us a certain instinct that makes us always tend toward and aim at that union in which all our happiness consists.

Carry out all your tasks with humility and confidence in God

The humility that does not produce generosity is undoubtedly false, for true humility, after it has said, "I can do nothing; I am only absolute nothingness," suddenly gives place to generosity of spirit, which says, "There is nothing and there can be nothing that I am unable to do, so long as I put all my confidence in God, who can do all things." And so, buoyed up by this confidence, it courageously undertakes to do all that is commanded.

But notice that I say "all that is commanded" or counseled, however difficult it may be: I can assure you that humility would not consider it impossible to work miracles if commanded to do so. For if the humble person sets himself to the execution of the command in simplicity of heart, God will work a miracle rather than fail in giving him the power to accomplish what he attempts, because he undertakes it not relying on his own strength, but on the gifts that God has bestowed on him. And so the humble person reasons thus with himself: "If God calls me to a state of perfection so high that in this life there is none higher, what can prevent my attaining to it, since I am well assured that He who has begun the work of my perfection will finish it?"[9]

But take note that all this is done without any presumption, for such confidence as I have described does not make us less on our guard for fear of failing. On the contrary, it renders us all the more watchful over ourselves, more vigilant and careful to do whatever may serve for our advancement in perfection.

Humility does not consist only in mistrust of ourselves, but also in confidence in God. Indeed mistrust of ourselves and of our own strength produces confidence in God; and of this confidence is born that generosity of spirit of which we are speaking.

The Blessed Virgin, our Lady, gives us a striking example of this in the words "Behold the handmaid of the Lord; be it done unto me according to thy word."[10]

[9] Cf. Phil. 1:6.

[10] Luke 1:38.

For in calling herself "the handmaid of the Lord," she makes the greatest act of humility possible. In opposition to the praises bestowed on her by the angel when he tells her that she shall be the mother of God and that the child who shall be born of her shall be called the Son of the Most High — the greatest dignity one could ever imagine — she brings forward her own lowliness and unworthiness: "Behold the handmaid of the Lord."

Yet observe that as soon as she has paid this debt to humility, she instantly makes an act of perfect generosity: "Be it done unto me according to thy word." "It is true," she would say, "that I am not in any respect capable of this grace, considering what I am, in and of myself; but since what is good in me is of God, and since what you tell me is His most holy will, I believe that it can and will be done." And therefore without hesitation she says, "Be it done unto me according to thy word."

Let your contrition be sincere and generous

It is likewise for lack of this generosity that so very few acts of true contrition are made. This is because, after having humbled and abased ourselves before the divine Majesty in consideration of our grievous infidelities, we do not go on to make this act of confidence, reviving our courage by the assurance that the divine Goodness will give us grace to be henceforth faithful to Him, and to conform more perfectly to His love. After this act of confidence, we ought instantly to make an act of generosity, saying, "Since I am fully assured that the grace of God will never fail me, I will also believe that He will not permit me to fail in conforming to that grace."

But you may reply, "If I fail grace, it will also fail me." That is true. "Who, then, shall assure me that I, who have so often failed to conform to grace in the past, shall not fail in the future?"

I answer that generosity makes the soul say boldly and without fear, "No, I will never again be unfaithful to God." And because the soul feels that this resolution is firmly fixed in the heart, it fearlessly sets itself to do all that it knows can render itself pleasing to God, without any exception whatsoever. And undertaking all, the soul believes that it can do all, not of itself, but in God, in whom the soul places all its confidence, and for whom it undertakes all that it is commanded or advised to do.

Never doubt your capability of carrying out your duties

You ask me, however, if we are never permitted to doubt our capability of doing the things that we are commanded to do. I reply that generosity of spirit never permits us to entertain the slightest doubt on the subject. In order that you may understand this better, you must distinguish, as I have often told you, between the higher part of our soul and the lower. When I say that generosity will not allow us to doubt, I am speaking with regard to our higher part, for it is quite possible that the lower part of our soul may be full of these doubts, and may experience great difficulty in accepting the charge or employment that is given to us. But the generous soul pays no heed to any such considerations, and simply sets itself to work to fulfill this charge without saying a single word or giving the slightest evidence of its feeling of incapacity.

We, on the contrary, are eager to show that we are very humble, and that we have a very poor estimation of ourselves, and so on. This is anything but true humility, which never permits us to resist the judgment of those whom God has given to us for our guidance.

In my book the *Introduction*[11] I have given an example that is to the point, and very remarkable; it is that of King Ahaz.[12] When he had been reduced to great misery by the fierce war made upon him by two other kings who had besieged Jerusalem, God commanded the prophet Isaiah to go and console him in His name, promising him that he should gain the victory and triumph over his enemies. Moreover, Isaiah told him that, as a proof of the truth of what he had promised, he was to "ask of God a sign, either in the heavens or earth," and it would be given him. Then Ahaz, distrusting the goodness and liberality of God, answered, "I will not do it, because I am not willing to tempt God." But the miserable man did not say this because of the honor in which he held God; on the contrary, he refused to honor Him, seeing that God on that occasion willed to be glorified by miracles, and Ahaz would not ask for one. Ahaz offended God by refusing to obey the prophet sent to him by God to intimate His will.

We must, then, never doubt for a moment our power of doing what we are commanded to do.

[11] *Introduction to the Devout Life*, Part 3, ch. 5.

[12] Isa. 7:3-12.

You can now understand sufficiently what this spirit of strength and generosity is. It banishes by its presence all the little follies and softnesses that only serve to hinder us on our way and prevent us from making progress in perfection. These softnesses are nourished by the idle reflections that we make about ourselves, chiefly when we have stumbled in our path by committing some fault. I say "stumbled," for here, by the grace of God, we do not fall outright; that has not yet occurred among us; but we stumble, and then, instead of quietly humbling ourselves and rising up again courageously, as I have said, we begin to dwell too much upon the thought of our wretchedness, and to lament over ourselves. "Alas!" we cry, "how miserable I am! I am fit for nothing!" From that we pass on to discouragement, which makes us exclaim, "Oh no! You must not hope for anything from me again; I shall never do any good; you are wasting time in speaking to me," and we sink to a state where we would almost rather be left to ourselves, as if it were fully recognized that nothing could be done with us.

Ah! How different is all this from the behavior of the generous soul, who, as we have said, holds in high estimation the good gifts with which God has endowed it. Such a soul is never dismayed, either by the difficulties of the road that it has to traverse, or by the greatness of the work it is called upon to perform, or by the length of time that it must give to it, or finally, by the delay in the progress of the work undertaken.

4

Obey those placed in authority over you

(from Conference X)

The obedience due to those superiors whom God has set over us to rule us is just and necessary, and ought to be rendered with an entire submission of our understanding and will. We practice this obedience of the understanding when, being commanded to do anything, we accept and approve the command, not only with the will but also with our understanding, approving and esteeming the thing commanded, and judging it better than any other thing that we could have been commanded on that occasion. When we have reached this point, we love to obey so much that we have an insatiable desire to be commanded, in order that all that we do may be done from obedience.

This is the obedience of the perfect. It is a pure gift from God, or else it is acquired with much time and labor, by means of a series of acts, often repeated and earnestly effected, by means of which we form the habit of obedience. Our natural inclination always leads us to wish to command, and makes us dislike to obey, and yet it is certain that we have a great capacity for obeying, and perhaps none at all for commanding.

Ordinary obedience has three conditions. The first is *acceptance* of the thing that we are commanded to do; we are to bend our will gently to it, loving to be commanded; for to have no one to command us is not the way to make us become truly obedient, any more than living alone in a desert is the way to become meek. Cassian relates that when he was in the desert, he sometimes became angry, and that when he took up a pen to write and found that it would not mark, he threw it away.[13] Thus, he says, living alone is of no avail, because we carry our anger about with us. Virtue is a good belonging to the self that does not depend on its contrary.

The second condition of obedience is *promptitude*, to which is opposed spiritual sloth or sadness, for it seldom happens that a soul in sadness does a thing promptly and diligently. In theological language, sloth is called spiritual sadness, and as such it prevents us from yielding brave and prompt obedience.

[13] John Cassian (c. 360-435; monastic writer), *The Institutes*, Bk. 8, ch. 18.

The third condition of obedience is *perseverance*; for it is not enough to accept the command and execute it for a certain space of time, if we do not persevere in so doing, for it is this perseverance that wins the crown.[14]

Admirable examples of perseverance are to be found everywhere. There have been monks who throughout their whole lives have, with incredible patience, persevered in doing only one kind of work.

One such is the good Father Jonas, who, besides gardening, never did anything in his life but make mats, and who was so much accustomed to this occupation that he continued it with the shutters closed while he prayed and meditated, the one occupation not interfering with the other.[15] At last they found him dead, his legs crossed and his mat stretched above them. He died doing what he had been doing all his life.

It is an act of great humility to go on all our lives doing from obedience one same and mean work, since we are often tempted to think we are quite capable of greater things.

[14] Cf. Matt. 10:22; 24:13; 2 Tim. 4:7-8.

[15] See *Paralipomena*, ch. 12, sections 29-30 in *Pachomian Koinonia*, trans. Armand Veilleux, vol. 2 (Kalamazoo, MI: Cistercian Publications, 1981), 53-55.

Persevere in your obedience

Now, this third condition is the most difficult of all, on account of the levity and inconstancy of the human spirit. For at one moment, we love to do a thing, and the next, we will not even look at it. If we were to follow all the motions of our spirit, and if it were possible to do so without scandal or dishonor, we would see nothing but change. So extravagant is this inconstancy of the human mind that one moment, we wish to be in one condition, and the next, we seek another. But we must bring the strength of our first resolutions to bear upon this inconstancy, so as to arrest it, and to live an equable life amid the diversities of our own feelings and of what happens around us.

Now, in order to increase our love for obedience, when we are tempted to disobedience, we must represent to ourselves the excellence, beauty, and merit of obedience, as well as its utility, so as to encourage ourselves to hold firm. This applies, however, to souls not yet well grounded in obedience; but when it is merely a question of simple disinclination and dislike of the thing we are commanded to do, we must just make an act of love and then set to work. Even our Lord in His

Passion shrank with an unspeakable horror and a mortal loathing from the pains of death. He says so Himself,[16] but with the fine point of His spirit, He was resigned to the will of His Father. All the rest was only the struggle of nature.

Obedience is so excellent a virtue that our Lord wished to direct the whole course of His life by it. He tells us often that He came not to do His own will, but the will of His Father;[17] and the Apostle says that He "made Himself obedient unto death, even the death of the Cross."[18] He was pleased to add to the infinite merit of His perfect charity the infinite merit of a perfect obedience.

Obedience takes precedence of charity, because obedience comes under justice, as again it is better to pay our debts than to give alms. Hence it is better to obey than to perform an act of charity of our own choice.

[16] Mark 14:34-36.

[17] John 4:34; 5:30; 6:38.

[18] Phil. 2:8.

5

Be patient as you seek perfection

(from Conference X)

We must all make allowances for one another's faults, and must not be at all put out when we come across them. If, for a time, we ourselves go on quietly without falling into any fault, another time will come when we shall find ourselves failing continually, and committing considerable imperfections.

However, we must profit from these, on account of the humiliation that they will bring upon us. We must suffer with patience the delay in our perfection, while always cheerfully doing what we can for our advancement therein.

Oh, how happy are those who, if made to wait all their lives, never grow weary of waiting! I say this for the sake of many who, having the desire to attain perfection by acquiring virtues, would like to have them all at once, as if perfection consisted only in desiring it. It would indeed be a fine thing if we could become humble as soon as we desired it, and without any more trouble. We must accustom ourselves to seek the attainment of our perfection by the usual paths, in tranquillity of heart, doing all that is in our power to acquire virtues, by our fidelity in practicing each of them according to our condition and vocation. But we must be content to wait regarding whether we shall attain the result of our aims sooner or later, leaving that to Divine Providence, which will not fail to console us at the appointed time. And even if that should not be until the hour of our death, we ought to be satisfied, so long as we fulfill our duty by always doing all that depends on us and all that is in our power.

We shall have quite soon enough what we desire, whenever we have it, and whenever it pleases God to give it to us. Waiting and resignation are very necessary, for the want of them disturbs the soul greatly. We must be contented to know that we are doing our duty regarding those who are over us, not seeking for any satisfaction or knowledge of things in particular, but walking blindfolded, as it were, in firm reliance on the Providence of God, even in the midst of the desolation, fears, gloom, and every other sort of cross that it may please Him to send us. Give yourself up, then, wholly and completely to His guidance, without any reserve or exception whatever, and leave Him to act, confiding all the care of body and soul to His goodness, remaining always completely resigned, composed, and resting in God, under the guidance of those in authority over you, without any care but to obey.

6

Be modest in your bearing

(from Conference IX)

A great saint wrote to one of his disciples, telling him to lie down at night as in the presence of God, exactly as anyone would have done if commanded by our Lord when He was on earth to lie down and sleep in His presence. It is true, the saint added, that you do not see Him and cannot hear the command that He is giving you, but nonetheless you should act as if you saw and heard Him, since He is truly present and guards you while you sleep.

O my God, how modestly and devoutly we should lie down to rest if we saw Thee! Doubtless, we should fold our arms upon our breast with the deepest devotion.

Religious modesty, then, keeps us in subjection at every moment of our lives, because the angels are always present as well as God Himself, for whose eyes we practice modesty.

This virtue is also much recommended on account of the edification of our neighbor. I assure you that a simple and modest exterior has converted many, as in the case of St. Francis,[19] who passed once through a town with such great modesty in his deportment that, although he did not speak a single word, a great number of young men followed him, attracted only by this, and desiring to be instructed by him.

A modest demeanor is a silent sermon; it is a virtue that St. Paul recommends most especially to the Philippians, saying, "Let your modesty be known to all men."[20] And when he tells his disciple St. Timothy that "a bishop must be adorned,"[21] he means not with rich clothing but with modesty, so that by his modest bearing, he may encourage all to approach him, avoiding alike rusticity and levity in such a way that, while giving liberty to worldlings to come to him, they may not think that he is worldly like them.

Now, the virtue of religious modesty observes three things: time, place, and person. For, tell me, would not one who was unwilling to show more cheerfulness in

[19] Probably St. Francis of Assisi (c. 1181-1226), the founder of the Franciscan Order; or possibly St. Francis Xavier (1506-1552), Jesuit missionary to the East Indies and Japan, who was canonized in 1622. — ED.

[20] Phil. 4:5.

[21] 1 Tim. 3:2.

recreation than out of recreation be very unsociable? There are gestures and behavior that would be unseemly out of recreation, but are not at all so at that time; so those who would laugh and relieve their mind in the midst of serious occupations, as they may very reasonably do at recreation, would they not be considered frivolous and giddy?

We must also take into consideration place, persons, the circle of which we may form part, and most especially the condition of the person. The modest demeanor of a woman of the world is not the same as that of a nun; a young lady in the world who kept her eyes lowered as do nuns would not be approved, any more than nuns would be if they in this particular did not exceed persons in the world. A demeanor that would be modest in one man would not be so in another, on account of his rank; a gravity extremely suitable in an elderly person would be affectation in a younger one, to whom a lowlier and humbler modesty belongs.

7

Practice interior modesty

(from Conference IX)

As modesty of bearing controls the gestures and the deportment of the body, avoiding the contrary vices of levity and license, and of an excessively affected carriage, so in the same way, interior modesty maintains the powers of our souls in tranquillity and moderation, avoiding curiosity of the understanding, over which it chiefly exercises its control, and also retrenching from our will its innumerable desires, and directing it simply to that "one thing" that Mary chose, and which "shall not be taken away from her" — that is, the will to please God.[22]

Martha represents very well lack of control in the will, for she is too eager: she sets all the servants of the house to work; she goes hither and thither without pausing for a moment, so anxious is she to treat our Lord well; and she seems to think she will never have enough dishes prepared to entertain Him.

[22] Luke 10:42.

In the same way, the will that is not restrained by moderation flits from one subject to another, in order to stimulate itself to love God and to desire many means of serving Him, and yet so many things are not needed. It is better to cling to God like Mary Magdalene, sitting at His feet, asking Him to give us His love, than to be thinking how and by what means we can acquire it. This modesty keeps our will confined to the exercise of those means of advancement in the love of God that belong to our own particular vocation.

I have said that this virtue chiefly exercises its control over the understanding; this is because our natural curiosity is very hurtful and prevents us from ever knowing a thing perfectly, since we never take time enough to learn it thoroughly. It also avoids the vice that lies at the other extreme — namely, that stupidity and carelessness of mind that does not care to know what is necessary.

To achieve peace of mind, focus on God

Now, this subjection of the understanding is of great importance as regards our perfection. Otherwise, the will cannot properly cling to its object, because the understanding shows it the beauty of something else, and so draws it away.

Bees cannot rest as long as they have no queen. They flutter about incessantly, wandering hither and thither; there is scarcely any repose in the hive. But as soon as their queen is born, they all gather around her, and stay there, never leaving her except to go and gather their spoils at her command.

In like manner, our understanding and will, our passions and the faculties of our soul, like spiritual bees, have no repose until they have a queen — that is, until they have chosen our Lord for their Sovereign. Our senses never cease to wander curiously about, drawing our interior faculties after them, wasting themselves now on one subject, now on another. Thus we are in continual affliction of spirit, in continual restlessness, which destroy that peace and tranquillity of mind so necessary to us; and this is what is produced by a lack of control of the understanding and will.

But as soon as our souls have chosen our Lord for their sole and sovereign King, all our powers grow quiet, like chaste and mystic bees, cluster around Him, and never leave their hive, except for those exercises of fraternal charity that this sacred King commands them to practice. As soon as these are accomplished, they return to recollection and holy, desirable quiet, in order to distill and store up the honey of the sweet and holy thoughts and affections that they draw from His sacred presence. Thus they avoid extremes, cutting off, on the one hand, curiosity of the understanding by simple attention to God, and, on the other, stupidity and carelessness of mind by the exercises of charity that they practice toward their neighbor when required.

Follow your God-given path to perfection

I remember talking to two nuns of two different well-reformed orders. One of them, from having read the works of the blessed Mother Teresa of Avila, had learned to speak so much like her that you might have fancied her a little Mother Teresa. Indeed, she believed it herself, having so vivid a sentiment of what the saintly Mother did during her life that she felt as if she herself did it also, even so far as to have abstraction from the senses and suspension of the powers, just as she had read about the saint; and really she could talk about it all very well. There are others like her who, from having meditated a great deal on the lives of the saints Catherine of Siena and Catherine of Genoa,[23] think themselves to be second St. Catherines by imitation. Certainly these souls have, at any rate, the satisfaction of imagining themselves to be saints, although their satisfaction is vain.

The other nun whom I knew was of a very different temperament; never was she satisfied or at rest, because she was always seeking out and desiring some way and method for becoming perfect; and always, in spite of her exertions, she kept fancying that there must be some other means of arriving at perfection than that which she had been taught.

One of these nuns lived contented in her imaginary holiness, seeking and desiring nothing else; the other lived in discontent because the perfection she sought was hidden from her, and she was therefore always desiring something else.

Interior modesty keeps the soul in a state between these two extremes, in that happy mean of desiring to know what is necessary, and nothing more. Moreover, I must remind you that the exterior modesty of which we have already spoken greatly helps the interior, and

[23] St. Catherine of Genoa (1447-1510), mystic.

the acquisition of peace and tranquillity in the soul. The proof of this is that all the holy Fathers, who were especially given to prayer, judged that a well-regulated posture contributed greatly to its efficacy, such as kneeling with clasped hands or arms outstretched.

8

Learn modesty in speech

(from Conference IX)

A third kind of modesty concerns our words and our conversation. There are words that would be unsuitable at any other time than that of recreation, in which it is just and reasonable to relax our minds a little. Indeed, at recreation, anyone who would not talk, or allow others to talk, on any but lofty and sublime subjects would act improperly; for have we not said that propriety takes account of times, places, and persons?

On this point, I must tell you that I was reading the other day that St. Pachomius, when he first retired into the desert to lead a monastic life, had great temptations, and evil spirits often appeared to him in various manners. The writer of his life tells us that on one occasion, when St. Pachomius had gone into the forest to cut wood, a great troop of these infernal spirits came upon him, seeking to terrify him, ranging themselves in order of battle, like well-armed soldiers keeping guard, and crying out to one another, "Make way for the holy man!" St. Pachomius, at once recognizing this as a bravado of the Evil One, began to smile, saying, "Ah! You are laughing at me, but, please God! I shall be one."

Then the Devil, seeing that he could not entrap the saint by making him depressed, thought he would try to catch him on the side of levity, since he had laughed at his first attempt. He therefore fastened a quantity of great cords to a single leaf of a tree, and then a troop of demons took hold of the cords and began to pull at the leaf, pretending to make most violent efforts, crying out and sweating as if it were a work of immense difficulty. The saint, raising his eyes and seeing this folly, pictured in his mind our Lord crucified upon the tree of the Cross; and they, perceiving that the saint was occupying himself with the fruit of the tree and not the leaf, fled, covered with shame and confusion.[24]

"There is a time to laugh and a time to weep," and there is also "a time to speak and a time to keep silence,"[25] as this glorious saint shows us in these temptations. This holy modesty regulates our manner of speaking, so that it becomes pleasing, neither too loud

[24] St. Pachomius (c. 290-346), the founder of Christian communal monasticism. See *The First Greek Life of Pachomius*, 18-19 in *Pachomian Koinonia*, vol. 1, 309-310.

[25] Eccles. 3:4, 7.

nor too low, neither too slow nor too quick. It keeps us within the bounds of holy moderation, so that when others are speaking, we allow them to do so without interrupting them, for that partakes of loquacity, and yet we speak when it is our turn, so as to avoid rusticity and self-sufficiency, which are such hindrances to good conversation. Often, too, occasions arise in which it is necessary to say much without speaking, by our modesty, serenity, patience, and calmness.

9

Accept reproofs without bitterness

(from Conference IX)

We should receive correction without letting any sensitiveness or bitterness of heart remain in us. To prevent a feeling of anger from stirring within us, and to keep the blood from showing itself in our face is surely impossible. Happy, indeed, shall we be if we attain to this perfection a quarter of an hour before we die! But to maintain bitterness in our minds in such a way that after this feeling has passed we do not speak with the same confidence, gentleness, and calmness as before — oh, this we must take all pains to avoid!

You say that you do all in your power to drive away the feeling, but it remains all the same. I assure you that in all probability, you only drive away this feeling in the same way as the citizens of a town in which a riot breaks out at night disperse their seditious enemies. They do not actually drive them out of the town, so the enemies can still go about secretly from street to street, and at daybreak they spring out upon the inhabitants and remain the masters. You, indeed, drive away the feeling that you have about being corrected, but not so vigorously and completely as to prevent some little of it lurking secretly in some corner of your heart. You do not wish to have this feeling, yet you do not wish to yield your judgment, which makes you believe that the correction was made either improperly, or from temper or some such cause. Who cannot see that this rebel will fall on you and put you to utter confusion if you do not promptly drive him away?

Turn away from anger that persists

What, then, must we do at such a time? We must cling closely to our Lord, and speak to Him of something else.

But your feelings are not yet calmed down; they are still suggesting that you dwell upon the wrong done to you. Ah! This is not the time to bring your judgment into subjection, to make it believe and own that the correction is good and made properly! Oh no! That must be done after your soul is calmed and quieted, for while it is troubled, you must neither do nor say anything, but only remain firm and resolved not to yield to passion, whatever excuse you might have; for at such times excuses will never be wanting — indeed, they will come in crowds! — but we must not listen to a single one, however good it may seem to us. We must simply, as I have said, keep close to God, diverting our minds by speaking to Him of other things, after we have humbled and abased ourselves before His divine Majesty.

But take note of these words, which I am glad to insist upon on account of their utility. When you humble yourselves, it must be with a gentle and peaceful, not with a querulous and impatient, humility. Unfortunately, we offer to God acts of humility so much against the grain, and so unwilling, that they do not calm our minds and are fruitless. But if, on the contrary, we made these acts in the presence of the divine Goodness with a sweet confidence, we should rise up serene and calm, able easily to reject all those reasons that our private judgment and self-love suggest, and which are often, one may say habitually, unreasonable; and we should be ready to converse just as before with those who reproved or contradicted us.

You can easily, you say, so far overcome yourselves as to speak to these people, but if they do not reply as you would like, the temptation recurs. Well, all this proceeds from the evil of which we have already spoken.

What should it matter to you whether they speak to you in one way or another, provided that you do your duty?

Everyone dislikes reproof, even the saints

But, when all is said and done, there is no one who does not dislike reproof. St. Pachomius, after having lived a most perfect life in the desert for fourteen or fifteen years, had a revelation from God that he would win a great number of souls, and that many would flock to the desert to place themselves under his guidance. He already had several religious with him, and the first whom he had received was his own elder brother John. St. Pachomius, then, having received this revelation, immediately set to work to enlarge his monastery, adding many cells to it. His brother John, either not knowing his intention, or out of his great zeal for poverty, addressed a severe reproof to him one day, asking him if it was by building so great a monastery that he expected and wished to imitate our Lord, who "had nowhere to lay His head"[26] while on earth.

[26] Matt 8:20; Luke 9:58.

St. Pachomius, saint though he was, felt this reproof so keenly that he turned away, in order, if I am not mistaken, to conceal his annoyance. Then he went and threw himself on his knees before God, asking pardon for his fault, and lamenting that, after so many years spent in the desert, he should still, as he said, be so unmortified. His prayer was so fervent and so humble that he obtained the grace of never again being guilty of impatience.[27]

Even St. Francis, toward the close of his life, after so many ecstasies and loving unions with God, after having done so much for His glory, and after having conquered himself in so many ways, one day, when he was planting cabbages in the garden, being reproved by one of the brothers for not planting them well, was affected by such a strong movement of anger that an abusive word against the brother half-escaped his lips. He actually opened his mouth to pronounce it, but restrained himself instantly, and stooping to take up some of the manure that he was digging in with the cabbages, he cried, "Ah! wicked tongue, I will teach thee what it is

[27] See *The First Greek Life of Pachomius*, 15 in *Pachomian Koinonia*, vol. 1, 307.

to abuse thy brother"; then suddenly throwing himself on his knees, he entreated the brother to forgive him.[28]

Now, what right, I ask you, have we to be surprised at finding ourselves quick to anger, and ready to resent reproof and contradiction? We must follow the example of these saints, who instantly conquered themselves, the one having recourse to prayer, the other humbly asking pardon of his brother, and neither the one nor the other doing anything to foster his sensitiveness, but turning away from it and profiting by it.

You say that you accept the reproof cheerfully, that you approve of it and consider it to be just and reasonable, but that it causes you a certain shame and embarrassment, as having displeased the person who reproved you or given him cause for displeasure, and that this deprives you of confidence in approaching him, although you love the abjection that is the result of your fault. This proceeds from self-love. You are not, perhaps, aware that there is within us a certain monastery, in which self-love is the superior, and therefore imposes penances. Well, the embarrassment that you feel is the

[28] The incident actually happened to one of St. Francis's disciples, Barbarus. See Thomas of Celano, *Second Life of St. Francis*, ch. 95. — Ed.

penance that self-love imposes on you for the fault of having displeased someone, because, perhaps, he will not esteem you so much as he would have done if you had not committed this fault.

When administering reproof, be forbearing

I have said enough for those who receive the reproof; now I must say a word about those who give it. Besides these being obliged to use great discretion in choosing times and seasons and other conditions for giving it, they must also never be disappointed or offended to see that it is felt by those to whom they administer it; for it is very painful to anyone to be reproved.

10

Turn your attention to God

(from Conference IX)

You ask how you can succeed in raising your mind directly to God, without turning to the right or to the left. This question contains its own answer: you must do as you say — go straight to God, without looking to the right or to the left. That is not, however, what you ask, I see very well, but rather what you must do in order to fix your mind so steadfastly in God that nothing can weaken its hold or withdraw it from Him. For this two things are necessary: to die and to be saved, for after that, there will be no more separation, and your spirit will be indissolubly attached and united to its God.

But what can you do to prevent the smallest distraction from withdrawing your mind from God as it does? Realize that the smallest distraction does not withdraw your soul from God, for nothing withdraws us from God but sin; and our resolution, made each morning, to keep our soul united to God and attentive to His presence, keeps us always there, even when we are sleeping, since we sleep in the name of God and according to His most holy will. (It even seems as if His divine Goodness said to us, "Sleep and rest; meanwhile I will watch over you to guard and defend you from the 'roaring lion that goeth about seeking whom he may devour.' "[29] Have we not, then, good reason to lie down to rest modestly?)

The means of doing well all that we do is to be very attentive to the presence of God, for no one would offend Him if he remembered that God is watching him. Venial sins are unable to turn us aside from the path that leads to God. They will doubtless delay our progress a little, but they will not turn us aside; still less will simple distractions, and this I have said in the *Introduction*.[30]

As regards prayer, it is not less profitable to us or less pleasing to God when it is full of distractions; nay, it will perhaps be more useful to us than if we had much consolation in it, because there will be more labor — provided, however, that we are faithful in withdrawing from these distractions, and in refraining from dwelling upon them voluntarily.

It is the same with regard to the difficulty that we experience throughout the day in dwelling upon the

[29] 1 Pet. 5:8.

[30] *Introduction to the Devout Life*, Part 1, chs. 5, 22.

thought of God and of heavenly things — provided that we are careful to restrain our minds as far as possible from running after these flitting butterflies, as a mother restrains her child. If she sees the poor little one longing to run off after the butterflies, hoping to catch them, she holds him back and says, "My child, you will only exhaust yourself by running after these butterflies in the sun; you had much better stay with me." The child stays with her, indeed, until he sees another, after which he would be as eager to run as ever if his mother did not hold him back in the same way.

What, then, can we do except have patience and not weary of our labors, since they are undertaken for the love of God?

11

Simply love God

(from Conference IX)

If I am not mistaken, when we say that we cannot find God and that He seems so far away, we mean only that we cannot feel His presence. I have before observed that many people do not distinguish between God and the *feeling* of God, between faith and the *feeling* of faith, which is a very great defect. It seems to them that when they do not feel God, they are not in His presence, which is a mistake.

A person who was about to suffer martyrdom for God and yet did not actually think of Him, but rather of his pain, although the feeling of faith may be wanting, yet does not fail to merit because of his first resolution, and makes an act of great love. There is a difference between being in the presence of God and having the feeling of His presence. God alone can give us the latter; as to my giving you the means of acquiring this sentiment, it is an impossibility.

Do you ask what you must do in order to keep yourself always with the deepest reverence before God, as being most unworthy of this grace? There is nothing to do but just what you say: to remember that He is our God, and that we are His feeble creatures, all unworthy of this honor. St. Francis did this; he spent a whole night asking God: "Who art Thou, and who am I?"[31]

In short, if you ask me "What can I do to acquire the love of God?" I answer, "By willing to love Him." And instead of setting to work to try to find out how you can unite your soul to God, put the thing in practice by a continual application of your mind to Him, and I assure you that you will arrive much more quickly at your object by this means than by any other.

For the more we pour ourselves out, the less recollected we shall be, and the less capable of union with the divine Majesty, who wishes to have all we are without reserve. One actually finds souls who are so busy in thinking how they shall do a thing that they have no time to do it; and yet, in what concerns our perfection, which consists in the union of our soul with the divine Goodness, there is no question of knowing much, but of doing. It seems to me that those of whom we ask the road to Heaven are very right in answering us like those

[31] *Chronicles of the Brothers Minor*, Bk. 1, ch. 8.

who tell us that, in order to reach such a place, we must just go on putting one foot before the other, and that by this means, we shall arrive where we desire. Keep walking, we say to these souls so desirous of their perfection, walking the way of your vocation with simplicity, more intent on doing than on desiring; that is the shortest road.

Do not seek a ready-made way of perfection

But here I perceive a little artifice that you must allow me to reveal to you, without your being offended. You want me to teach you a sort of ready-made way of perfection, one that you have only to put your head into it, or put it on like a dress, and thus be perfect, without taking any trouble. You want me, I say, to give you a ready-made perfection, for what I tell you must be done is not pleasing to nature; it is not what we want. Certainly, if that were in my power I should be the most perfect man in the world; for if I could give perfection to others without their having to do anything, I assure you that I should take it first of all for myself! You fancy that perfection is an art of which, if you can only discover the secret, you will instantly obtain possession, without any trouble. Certainly this is a great mistake, for, in aspiring to union with the Beloved, there is no other secret than to do what we aspire to — that is, to labor faithfully in the exercise of divine love.

I wish you, however, to observe that when I say we must do this, I am always referring to the superior part of our soul, for as regards all the feelings of repugnance in the inferior part, we must pay no more heed to them than passersby do to the dogs they hear barking in the distance. Those who at a banquet try every dish, eating a little of each, so disorder their stomachs that they cannot sleep, and pass the night with the usual consequences of indigestion. So it is with those souls who wish to try all methods and means that may lead them to perfection, for their spiritual stomach not having sufficient heat to digest and put into practice so many methods, a certain discomfort and indigestion succeeds, which deprives them of that peace and serenity of mind in the presence of our Lord that is "the one thing needful," which Mary chose, and "which shall not be taken away from her."[32]

[32] Luke 10:42.

12

Continue to make good resolutions

(from Conference IX)

Let us pass on now to the other question — namely, what you can do to strengthen your resolutions and make them succeed? There is no better means than to put them into practice.

But you say that you are still so weak that, although you often make strong resolutions not to fall into the particular imperfection of which you want to cure yourself, no sooner does the occasion present itself than down you go.

Shall I tell you why we are still so weak? It is because we will not abstain from food that does not agree with us. It is as if a person who wished to be free from pains in the stomach were to ask a physician what he should do. The doctor replies, "Do not eat such and such food, because it brings you pain"; and yet the person will not abstain from it.

We do the same. For example, we should like to love reproof, and yet we obstinately cling to our own opinion. That is foolishness. You will never be strong enough to bear reproof courageously while you are nourishing yourself with the food of self-esteem. I wish to keep my soul recollected, and yet I will not restrain all sorts of idle thoughts: the two things are incompatible. Ah! How much I wish that I could be steadfast and regular in my religious exercises; at the same time I wish not to find them so trying — in fact, I want to find the work done for me. That cannot be in this life, for we shall always have to labor.

Do not be discouraged by your failures

We must make two equally firm resolutions: one, to be ready to see weeds growing in our garden; the other, to have the courage to see them pulled up, and to pull them up ourselves; for our self-love, which produces these miseries, will never die while we live.

Besides, to fall sometimes into venial sin does not make a weak soul, provided that we rise up quickly by turning our soul toward God and quietly humbling ourselves. We must not imagine that we can live without ever committing any sins, for only our Lady had that privilege. Certainly, even if venial sins retard our progress a little, as I have said before, they do not turn us aside from the way; one single look at God effaces them.

Lastly, I would have you know that we must never cease to make good resolutions, even though we may be well aware that, generally speaking, we do not carry them into effect — yes, even if we should see that it will be out of our power to do so when the opportunity offers. Indeed, we must make them with still more firmness than if we felt within ourselves courage enough to succeed in our enterprise, saying to our Lord: "It is true that I shall not have strength enough to do or to bear such and such a thing of myself, but 'I rejoice in my infirmity,' because it will be Thy 'strength' that will do it in me."[33]

Relying on this help, go forth courageously to the battle, and doubt not that you will gain the victory. Our Lord treats us as a good father and a good mother treat their child, who is allowed to walk alone as long as he is on the soft grass of a meadow, or some mossy carpet, because even if he were to fall, he could not do himself much harm; but on rough and dangerous roads they carry the little one tenderly in their arms.

[33] 2 Cor. 12:9-10.

Even the saints experience failures

We have often seen souls courageously sustaining great assaults, without being vanquished by their enemies, and yet afterward defeated in very slight combats. Why is this, if not that our Lord, seeing that they would not do themselves much harm by falling, has allowed them to walk alone, which He did not do when they were among the precipices of great temptations, from which His all-powerful hand extricated them.

St. Paula,[34] who so bravely renounced the world, quitting Rome and all its luxuries, and who could not even be shaken by her maternal affection for her children, so resolute was her heart in forsaking all for God — even she, after having effected these marvelous things, allowed herself to be overcome by the temptation of private judgment, which made her believe that she ought not to submit to the counsel of various holy persons who would have her give up some of her accustomed austerities, in which St. Jerome confesses that she was to blame.[35]

[34] St. Paula (347-404), Roman matron and ascetic.

[35] St. Jerome, *Letter* 108 to Eustochium, section 20.

In conclusion, let me observe that all that we have said here relates to delicate points of perfection, and therefore you must not be disappointed if you find that you have not yet attained to such perfection, since by the grace of God, you have the courage to wish to aim at it.

May Jesus ever live!

13

Love God simply

(from Conference XII)

Now, in the first place, it is necessary to understand what this virtue of simplicity is. You know that, generally speaking, we call a thing simple when it is not embroidered, lined, or of more than one color. For instance, we say, "That person is dressed very simply," when her dress is only of one material; "That is a simple dress" — I mean, with no trimming or lining that we can see, and no outside ornamentation.

Well, simplicity is nothing else than an act of pure and simple charity, having only one aim and end, which is to acquire the love of God; and our soul is simple when we have no other aim in all that we do or desire.

The well-known story of the two hostesses, Martha and Mary, who entertained our Lord, is most noteworthy for this very thing. Do you not see that although Martha's desire to show great hospitality to our Lord was laudable, yet she was reproved by that divine Master because she added another motive to the good object that made her so eager to serve Him? For, looking upon our Lord as man, and believing Him to be like ordinary human beings who cannot be satisfied with a simple meal of one dish, she bustled about, busy in the preparation of many, varied dishes. So, to the first pure aim of the love of God, she added many little secondary motives, for which she was reproved by our Lord: "Martha, Martha, thou art careful and art troubled about many things. But one thing is necessary. Mary hath chosen the best part, which shall not be taken away from her."[36]

This act of simple charity, then, which allows us to have no other aim in all our actions but the one desire of pleasing God, is Mary's part, which is alone necessary. This is simplicity, a virtue that is inseparable from charity, inasmuch as it looks straight to God, without ever permitting any admixture of self-interest. It would otherwise no longer be simplicity, for that virtue cannot endure any addition of creatures or any consideration of them. God alone finds place in it.

This virtue is Christian only. Pagans, even the most eloquent on the subject of the other virtues, knew nothing whatsoever of this virtue, any more than of humility. They wrote very well on magnanimity, liberality, and

[36] Luke 10:41-42.

constancy, but of simplicity and humility they have written nothing at all. Our Lord Himself came down from Heaven to make known to men both these virtues; without this, mankind would have remained ignorant of this doctrine that is so necessary. "Be ye wise as serpents," He said to His Apostles; but go still further, "be simple as doves."[37]

Learn from the dove to love God in simplicity of heart, having but one aim and object in all you do. Do not, however, only imitate the simple love of those birds in their having only one mate, for whom alone they do everything and whom alone they wish to please, but also imitate them in the simplicity with which they express and show their love. They do not practice little mincing ways, but only coo gently by the side of their mates, happy enough just to rest quietly in their presence.

Learn to banish care from your soul

Simplicity banishes from the soul that solicitous care which so needlessly urges many to seek out various exercises and means to enable them, as they say, to love

[37] Matt. 10:16.

God. And it seems to them that if they do not do all that the saints did, they cannot be content. Poor souls! They torment themselves about finding the art of loving God, not knowing that there is none except to love Him. They think that there is a certain art needed to acquire this love, which is really to be found only in simplicity.

In fact, there is no other art than to set ourselves to the work of loving Him, applying ourselves to the practice of those things that are pleasing to Him. This is the only means of finding and acquiring this holy love, provided that this practice is undertaken in simplicity, without trouble or solicitude. Simplicity embraces all the means that are prescribed to each of us, according to his vocation, for acquiring the love of God, so that it desires no other motive for acquiring or being incited to the quest for this love than itself. Otherwise it would not be perfectly simple; for simplicity cannot bear to concern itself about anything, however perfect, but the pure love of God, which is its single and only aim.

Be prudent but not cunning

Now, before proceeding further, I must correct a mistake with regard to this virtue, which lurks in the minds of many. They think that simplicity is contrary to prudence and that the two virtues are opposed to one another. This is not so, for the virtues never clash with each other. On the contrary, they are bound together in the closest union.

The virtue of simplicity is opposed and contrary to the vice of cunning, a vice from which arises all manner of deceit, craftiness, and duplicity. Cunning includes deceits, deceptions, and malice, and it is through cunning that we find out how to deceive the mind of our neighbor, and of those with whom we come into contact, so as to lead them on to the point for which we are scheming. Now, this point is to convince them that we have no other feeling in our heart but what is manifested in our words, nor any other knowledge about the subject in question. This is something that is absolutely contrary to simplicity, which requires that the interior should be wholly conformable to the exterior.

Let even your prudence be simple

I have been thinking that if I spoke of the simplicity of the dove, the wisdom of the serpent would be sure to be thrown in my face. Many people have asked what was the serpent from which our Lord wished us to learn wisdom.

Putting aside all other answers that may be given to this question, let us now consider the words of our Lord, "Be ye wise as serpents," who, when they are attacked, expose their whole bodies in order to preserve their heads. We, too, ought to do likewise, exposing everything to danger when necessary, in order to preserve within us, safe and untouched, our Lord and His love. For He is our "Head," and we are His "members,"[38] and that is the prudence that ought to be joined to our simplicity.

You must remember that there are two kinds of prudence — the natural and the supernatural. As for the natural, it must be thoroughly mortified as not being at all good, suggesting to us many considerations and much forethought, which are quite unnecessary and which keep our minds far from simplicity.

The true virtue of prudence ought to be really practiced, the more so because it is like a spiritual salt that gives taste and savor to all the other virtues. But it ought to be practiced in such a manner that the virtue of

[38] Cf. 1 Cor. 12:27; Col. 1:18.

simple confidence shall surpass all the others. For you ought to have a perfectly simple confidence, which will make you repose in the arms of your heavenly Father and of your dearest mother, our Lady, assured of the continual protection of that most loving care, since you are gathered together for the glory of God and the honor of the most Blessed Virgin.

Remain outwardly calm

In saying that simplicity requires the interior to be in conformity with the exterior, I do not mean to say that in the case of our emotions, we ought to make an outward demonstration of passions that may be inwardly disturbing us; for it is not, as some think, contrary to simplicity to show a calm exterior at such times.

We must always discriminate between what affects the higher part of our soul and what affects the lower part. It is true that sometimes, on meeting with a reproof or any kind of contradiction, we are inwardly much disturbed, but this emotion does not proceed from our will. All the trouble goes on in the lower part of our soul; the higher does not consent to it at all, but approves, accepts, and values this reproof or contradiction.

We have said that simplicity aims steadily at acquiring the love of God. Now, the love of God requires us to restrain our feelings, to mortify and to subdue them, and this is why it does not require us to make any outward demonstration of them. It is, then, no want of simplicity to keep a calm exterior when we are inwardly moved and agitated.

14

Be untroubled by public opinion

(from Conference XII)

Consideration of what will be said or thought of you is contrary to simplicity. This virtue, as we have said, looks only to pleasing God, not creatures at all, except insofar as the love of God requires it. After the simple soul has done the action that it considers it ought to do, it thinks no more about it. And if it should occur to the person to wonder what will be said or thought of him, the soul checks the thought instantly, because it will allow nothing to divert it from its one aim, namely, of dwelling on the thought of God alone, that it may love Him more and more. The consideration of creatures has no power to move the soul, for it refers all to the Creator.

We must not perpetually fear trouble, either for ourselves or for others, for trouble of itself is not sin. If I know that by going into certain society, I shall expose myself to the risk of hearing something said to me that will trouble and disturb me, I ought not to avoid going into it; but I ought to go, armed with confidence in divine protection, certain that it will strengthen me so that I may overcome my own nature, against which I desire to make war. This conflict goes on only in the lower part of our soul. That is why we must not be at all astonished when it has no results. I mean, of course, when we do not consent to what it suggests, for in such a case, we must avoid it.

But where do you think this trouble comes from, if not from a want of simplicity and especially because we often waste our time in conjecturing "What will they say? What will they think?" instead of thinking only of God and of what will render us more pleasing to His goodness? "But if I say such and such a thing, I shall be in more trouble than before I said it." Well, if you do not wish to say it, and if it is not necessary, seeing that you have no need of instruction upon it, make up your mind quickly and waste no time in considering whether you ought to say it or not. We are not meant to give an hour's consideration to all the small actions of our life.

And if you are still in trouble, it is only because you are unmortified; for why should I say what will be of no use to me, leaving out what might mortify me? Simplicity, as we have already said, seeks nothing but the pure love of God, which is nowhere to be found so certainly as in self-mortification. In proportion to the growth of that mortification will be our nearer and nearer approach to that place where we shall find His divine love.

Simplicity does not meddle with what others are doing or will do; it thinks of itself. But even as regards itself, it dwells only upon really necessary thoughts, and always turns quickly away from any others. This virtue has a close affinity to humility, which does not allow us to have a bad opinion of anyone but ourselves.

You ask how you must observe simplicity in conversation and recreation. I reply: as in all other actions, although in this particular one there should be a holy freedom and frankness in conversing upon such subjects as serve to foster a spirit of joy and recreation. We should be quite unaffected in conversation, but at the same time not inconsiderate, for simplicity always follows the rule of the love of God. But should we happen to say some little thing that seems to us not to be received as we would wish, we must not on that account waste time in weighing and searching into all our words. No, it is indeed self-love, undoubtedly, which makes us inquire so closely whether our words and actions have been well received or not.

Be as simple as a child

Holy simplicity does not run after its words and actions, but leaves the result of them to Divine Providence, on whom it absolutely depends. It turns neither to the right nor to the left, but simply pursues its path straight and direct. If in that path it meets with any opportunity of practicing some particular virtue, it makes careful use of it as an appropriate means toward attaining its perfection, which is the love of God. But it is not eager in seeking out those opportunities, although, at the same time, it does not despise them. Simplicity troubles about nothing, but remains modest and tranquil in its certainty that God knows its desire, which is to please Him; that is enough.

"But how is it possible to reconcile two such contrary propositions? We are told, on the one hand, that we are to be most careful about our advancement in perfection, and, on the other, that we are forbidden to think about it at all!" Please observe here the misery of human nature, which can never stop short at the golden mean, but, generally speaking, runs to extremes. This defect we inherit from our mother Eve, for she did much the same when the evil spirit tempted her to eat of the forbidden fruit. She said that God had forbidden them to touch it,[39] instead of saying that He had forbidden them to eat it. You were never told not to think at all about your advancement, but that you were not to think about it anxiously.

It is, indeed, absolutely true that your well-being depends on your allowing yourself to be guided and governed by the Spirit of God without reserve. This is the aim of that true simplicity which our Lord recommends so highly. "Be ye simple as doves," He says to His Apostles; but He does not stop there, saying also to them, "Unless you become simple as little children, you shall not enter into the kingdom of my Father."[40]

A child, when very young, is in a state of such simplicity that he has no knowledge of anything but of his mother. He has only one love, which is for his mother; and in that love only one aim and desire — his mother's breast; when he is upon that beloved breast, he wants nothing more.

The soul that has attained perfect simplicity has only one love, which is for God. In this love it has only

[39] Gen. 3:3.

[40] Matt. 18:3.

one aim — to rest upon the bosom of the heavenly Father, and there to abide like a beloved child, leaving all care of itself to that good Father. This soul is anxious about nothing except to maintain this holy confidence; it is not even disquieted by any desires for those virtues and graces that seem to it necessary. It is true that such a soul never neglects any good opportunity that it meets with on its way, but it does not hunt about eagerly for means of perfecting itself other than those that are prescribed.

Now, what is the use of these disquieting, eager desires for virtues that there is no need for us to practice? Gentleness, love of our abjection, humility, sweet charity, cordiality toward our neighbor, and obedience are virtues whose practice ought to be common to us all, and they are all the more necessary insofar as we have frequent occasions of practicing them. But as for constancy, magnanimity, and similar virtues that we may never be required to practice, we certainly need not trouble ourselves about them; we shall be nonetheless magnanimous or generous on that account.

You ask me how souls, attracted in prayer to this holy simplicity and perfect abandonment of themselves to God, ought to conduct themselves in all their actions?

I reply that not only in prayer, but in the conduct of their whole life, they ought to walk invariably in a spirit of simplicity. They should abandon and submit their whole soul, their actions, and their successes to the good pleasure of God, by a love of perfect and entire confidence, relying wholly on the mercy and care of that eternal love which Divine Providence has for them. For this end, let them keep their soul steadfastly in this path, without allowing it to waste its powers in continual self-inspection, for the purpose of seeing what they are doing or if they are satisfied.

Alas! Our own satisfactions and consolations do not satisfy God; they only feed that miserable love and care of ourselves that is quite independent of God and the thought of Him.

Certainly children, whom our Lord tells us should be our model of perfection, are, generally speaking, quite free from care, especially in the presence of their fathers and mothers. They cling to them, without turning to consider their satisfactions or their consolations. These they presume in good faith, and enjoy in simplicity, without any curiosity whatsoever as to their causes or effects. Love occupies them sufficiently without their doing anything else.

Those whose one desire is to please the heavenly Lover, have neither the inclination nor the leisure to turn back upon themselves; their minds tend continually in the direction in which love carries them.

15

Abandon yourself wholly to God

(from Conference XII)

St. Francis, sending his children out on their travels into desolate places, gave them this advice instead of money and provisions: "Cast thy care upon the Lord, and He shall sustain thee."[41] I say the same to you: cast your hearts, aspirations, anxieties, and affections upon the paternal bosom of God, and He will guide you. He will carry you wherever His love would have you go.

Let us hear and follow the voice of the divine Savior, who, like the most excellent psalmist, sings the sovereign features of His love from the tree of the Cross. He concludes them as follows: "Father, into Thy hands I commend my spirit."[42] After that has been said, what is left but to breathe forth our last breath and die of love, living no longer ourselves, but Jesus Christ living in us?[43] Then the anxieties of our heart will cease — anxieties

[41] Ps. 54:23 (RSV= Ps. 55:22).

[42] Luke 23:46; Ps. 30:6 (RSV = Ps. 31:5).

[43] Gal. 2:20.

proceeding from desires suggested by self-love and tenderness for ourselves, which make us secretly so eager in the pursuit of our own satisfaction and perfection.

Embarked, then, in the exercises of our vocation, carried along by the wind of this simple and loving confidence, without being aware of it, we shall make the very greatest progress; without moving, we shall advance; and without stirring from our place, we shall draw nearer and nearer to home, as do those who sail on the high seas with favorable winds. Then, too, every possible event and variety of accident that may happen will be received calmly and peacefully.

For what is there that can disturb or move those who are in the hands of God and rest upon His bosom — those who have abandoned themselves to His love and have resigned themselves to His good pleasure? Whatever may happen, without wasting time in philosophizing upon the causes, reasons, and motives of events, they utter from their heart the holy acquiescence of our Savior: "Yea, Father, for so hath it seemed good in Thy sight."[44] Then we shall be all steeped, as it were, in sweetness and gentleness toward all our neighbors, for

[44] Matt. 11:26.

we shall look upon these souls as resting in our Savior's Heart.

Alas! They who regard their neighbor in any other way run the risk of not loving him with purity, constancy, and impartiality. But beholding him in that divine resting place, who would not love him, bear with him, and be patient with his imperfections? Who would find him irritating or troublesome?

Well, your neighbor is there, in the Heart of the Savior, there as so beloved and so lovable that the divine Lover dies of love for him!

Then, again, the natural love of our family, good manners, courtesy, affinity, sympathy, and kindliness will be purified and reduced to the perfect obedience of the all-pure love of the divine good pleasure. And, assuredly, the highest good, and the highest happiness of souls aspiring to perfection, should be to have no desire whatsoever to be loved by creatures, except with that love of charity which makes us feel an affection for our neighbor, and for everyone in his proper order, as our Lord desires.

16

Do not seek special crosses or privileges

(from Conference XXI)

I was speaking one day to an excellent nun, who asked me if, wishing to go to Communion more often than the rest of the community, she might ask permission of the superior to do so. I told her that if I were a religious, I think I should not ask to be allowed to communicate more often than my brethren, nor to wear sackcloth, a hair-shirt, or an iron girdle, nor to perform extraordinary fasts, nor anything of that kind. I should content myself with following in all respects the ways of the community.

If I were in strong health I would not eat four times a day; but if I were asked to take these four meals, I would do so, and say nothing. If I were in feeble health, and yet was told to eat only once a day, I would obey without thinking whether I was in feeble health or not.

I wish for few things, and what I do wish for, I wish for but slightly. I have scarcely any desires, but if I could begin my life over again, I would have none at all. If God came to me, I would also go to Him; but if He did not will to come to me, I would stay where I was, and would not go to Him. I say, then, that we must neither ask for anything nor refuse anything, but must leave ourselves in the arms of Divine Providence, without busying ourselves with any desires, except to will what God wills of us.

St. Paul practiced this self-abandonment most excellently at the very moment of his conversion. For when our Lord had smitten him with blindness, he cried out instantly, "Lord, what wilt Thou have me to do?"[45] and from that time forth, he continued in absolute dependence upon the will and commands of God. Our whole perfection lies in the practice of this. The same St. Paul, writing to one of his disciples, forbids him, among other things, to allow his heart to be preoccupied with any desire, so well did the great Apostle know the danger of this failing.

You say, "We must not, then, desire virtues, although our Lord says, 'Ask, and it shall be given to you.' "[46] When I say that you must ask for nothing and desire nothing, I am speaking of earthly things; as for virtues,

[45] Acts 9:6.

[46] Matt. 7:7; Luke 11:9.

we may, of course, ask for them, and in asking for the love of God, we include all, for the love of God contains them all.

But, you say, as regards external matters, may we not desire mean and lowly offices and employments, because they are more laborious and troublesome, and give us more opportunities of humbling ourselves for God's sake? David said that he would rather "be abject in the house" of the Lord than be great "among sinners";[47] and "It is good, O Lord," he says, "that Thou hast humbled me that I may learn Thy justifications."[48] Nevertheless, such a desire is very suspicious, and may spring from merely human considerations.

How do you know whether, having desired mean offices, you will have strength to accept the humiliations that will meet you in them at every turn, as well as the bitterness, weariness, and disgust that may come upon you? For although you may at the present moment feel strength sufficient to endure mortifications and humiliations, how do you know that you will always have it?

[47] Ps. 83:11 (RSV = Ps. 84:10).

[48] Ps. 118:71 (RSV = Ps. 119:71).

In short, a desire for any special occupations, whatever they may be, whether mean or honorable, must always be regarded in the light of a temptation. It is always best to desire nothing, but to hold ourselves in readiness to receive whatever obedience may impose upon us. Whether these duties, so imposed, be exalted or lowly, I should accept them humbly without saying a word, unless questioned on the subject, when I should reply simply and truthfully, saying just what I thought.

Imitate St. Peter's mother-in-law

You wonder how we can practice this holy indifference when sickness comes upon us. I find in the holy Gospels a perfect model in St. Peter's mother-in-law.[49] That good woman, lying sick of a great fever, practiced many virtues, but the one that I admire the most is her absolute self-surrender to the Providence of God and the care of her superiors.

She was stricken with fever, and still was tranquil and peaceful, without any disquietude about herself, and causing none to those who were with her. Yet we all

[49] Matt. 8:14-15; Luke 4:38-39.

know what is the natural condition of a fever patient; the burning restlessness makes repose impossible and is accompanied by a thousand other discomforts. Now, this great surrender that our sick woman made of herself into the hands of her superiors prevented her from being the least anxious or uneasy as to her health or as to the probability of her recovery; she was content to bear her malady with sweetness and patience.

Oh, how happy was this good woman! Certainly she deserved to be well cared for, as indeed she was by the Apostles, who, without any solicitation on her part, provided for her cure out of charity and compassion for all that she suffered. This is because charity is much stronger and much more assiduous than mere natural affection.

This dear invalid knew very well that our Lord was at Capernaum, and that He was healing the sick, yet she did not fret and disquiet herself, trying to send someone to let Him know that she was suffering. But, what is more admirable still, she saw Him enter her house, where He saw her and she saw Him, too, and even then, she did not say a single word to Him about her illness to arouse His pity for her, nor did she hasten to touch Him so that she could be healed.

This anxiety that people exhibit about their sufferings and illnesses (to which not only persons in the world, but also religious are subject) springs from a disordered self-love. But Peter's mother-in-law, despite her fever, did not make anything of her illness, nor did she feel moved to speak of it. She endured it without worrying about whether others felt sorry for her or were trying to obtain her cure. She was content that God and her superiors knew about it.

She saw our Savior enter her house as the sovereign Physician, yet so little was she occupied about her cure that she did not even think of Him in this capacity. In her eyes, He was her God alone, to whom she belonged in health and in sickness, being as content to be sick as to be in perfect health.

How many would have used little arts and subterfuges that they might be healed by our Lord, and would have said that they only asked for health that they might serve Him better, fearing that He might need something done that in their sickness they could not do! But this good woman had no such thought and showed her perfect resignation in not even asking to be healed. I do not, however, say that we may not very justly ask this of our Lord, who alone can give us this boon, but it must be with this condition: *if such is His will.* For we should always say, "Thy will be done."[50]

It is not enough to be sick or afflicted because God wills it; we must be so as He wills, when He wills, for as long as He wills, and exactly in the manner in which it pleases Him; neither choosing nor rejecting any sickness or affliction, however mean and abject it may seem to us, for sickness and affliction without abjection often inflate the heart instead of humbling it! When we have any kind of pain or ill without honor, or when dishonor, degradation, and abjection are themselves the very ills from which we suffer, what opportunities arise for exercising patience, humility, modesty, and sweetness of mind and heart!

So let us be most careful, like this good woman, to keep our hearts submissive, profiting, as she did, by our maladies, for "she rose up" as soon as our Lord had driven away the fever, and "ministered to Him."[51] In doing this, she certainly showed great virtue, and showed that she had profited by her sickness, for, being once rid of it, she desired only to use her health for the service of our Lord,

[50] Matt. 6:10.

[51] Matt. 8:15; Luke 4:39.

employing it for this purpose the very instant she had recovered it. Truly she was not like people in the world, who, after a few days' sickness, require weeks or months to recuperate.

17

Desire nothing, refuse nothing

(from Conference XXI)

Our Lord upon the Cross shows us how we must mortify our softness. When a burning thirst was consuming Him, He asked for nothing to drink, but simply made known His necessity, saying "I thirst." After this He made an act of perfect submission; and when someone offered Him, on the point of a lance, a sponge steeped in vinegar to slake His thirst, He moistened His blessed lips with it.[52] How wonderful! He knew that it was a beverage that would increase His suffering, yet He took it simply without showing any displeasure or disgust, to teach us with what submission we ought to take the remedies and nourishment presented to us when we are sick, without showing a great deal of repulsion and dissatisfaction, even though we may be doubtful whether they will do us any good.

Alas! When we are suffering even the very slightest inconvenience, we do just the very contrary to what our

[52] John 19:28-30.

gentle Master has taught us! For we never cease bewailing ourselves, and it seems as if we could not find enough people to whom to complain and recite our catalog of aches and pains. Our suffering, whatever it may be, is quite unique; what others may have to endure is not to be compared with it! We are too impatient and worried for words; nothing can be found to satisfy us. Truly, it is a sorrowful thing to see how little we imitate the patience of our Savior, who forgot His own grief and agonies, and did not try at all to make them known to men, contented that His heavenly Father, through obedience to whom He endured them, should look upon them, and that thus His wrath should be appeased toward that human nature for which He suffered.

Do you ask what I desire should remain most deeply engraved upon your mind, so that you may put it into practice? Ah, what shall I say, but those excellent words I have so often already recommended to you: *desire nothing, refuse nothing*. These words say it all, for they capture in a nutshell the practice of perfect indifference.

Look at the infant Jesus in the manger: He accepts poverty, nakedness, the company of brute beasts, all the inclemencies of the weather — all, in fact, that happens to Him by His Father's permission. We are never told that He stretched forth His little hands to His mother's breast. He left her to provide all that was necessary to Him, but, at the same time, He never refused the little comforts that she gave Him. He received the services of St. Joseph, the adoration of the kings and of the shepherds, all with equal indifference.

So, too, ought we to desire nothing and to refuse nothing, but to suffer and to receive with perfect evenness of mind all that the Providence of God may allow to happen to us. May God give us grace to do this.

Blessed be God!

Biographical note

St. Francis de Sales

1567-1622

A Doctor of the Church and the patron saint of writers, St. Francis de Sales was remarkable "not only for the sublime holiness of life which he achieved, but also for the wisdom with which he directed souls in the ways of sanctity."[53]

The eldest of thirteen children, Francis de Sales was born in 1567 to a noble family in the French-speaking Duchy of Savoy (an area straddling present-day eastern France and western Switzerland). He received a superb education in both France and Italy. Although intended by his father for a diplomatic career, St. Francis was ordained to the priesthood in the diocese of Geneva in 1593. Shortly thereafter, he was sent to the Chablais region of the Savoy on a mission to persuade those who had fallen under Calvinist influence to return to the practice of Catholicism. St. Francis spent four years laboring at this difficult task, during which he suffered

[53] Pope Pius XI, *Rerum omnium perturbationem*, 4.

many indignities. More than once he was thrown out of his lodgings and had to sleep in the open air. Many times he celebrated Mass in empty churches or continued preaching while the congregation walked out. Nevertheless, St. Francis's unflagging poise and kindness in this mission led to its eventual success. By the turn of the century, the majority of the area's inhabitants had returned to the Catholic faith.[54]

After his election as bishop of Geneva in 1602, St. Francis continued his apostolic efforts to win souls back to the Catholic Church. At the same time, he sought to build a broad community of devout persons within the Church who would live the life of Christian perfection in all their varied states and vocations.[55]

It was St. Francis's absolute conviction that "holiness is perfectly possible in every state and condition of secular life," whether one is male or female, rich or poor, single or married.[56] He expounded this view at length in his classic work *Introduction to the Devout Life*. This

[54] Ibid., 8.

[55] *Francis de Sales, Jane de Chantal: Letters of Spiritual Direction*, ed. Wendy M. Wright and Joseph F. Power (New York: Paulist Press, 1988), 23.

[56] Pius XI, *Rerum omnium perturbationem*, 13.

conviction permeates the advice he gave to the many persons from all walks of life to whom he gave spiritual direction, both in person and in letters renowned for their spiritual wisdom, their psychological insight, their graciousness, and what one scholar has called their "inspired common sense."[57]

Jane Frances Frémyot, Baroness de Chantal, is the most famous of those who came to St. Francis for spiritual direction. An aristocratic young widow with four children, she met St. Francis in 1604. In cooperation with her, St. Francis founded the Visitation of Holy Mary in Annecy in Savoy, a congregation for unmarried and widowed women who aspired to religious life but who were not sufficiently young, healthy, or free of family ties to enter one of the more austere women's orders of the day. The Visitation eventually developed into a cloistered religious order devoted to prayer and the cultivation of the "little virtues" St. Francis praised so highly. The order flourished during St. Francis's lifetime, and afterward. St. Jane de Chantal was herself canonized in 1751.

[57] Elisabeth Stopp, ed., *St. Francis de Sales: Selected Letters* (New York: Harper and Bros., 1960), 33-34.

After nearly thirty years of tireless labor on behalf of the Church and its members, St. Francis de Sales died of a cerebral hemorrhage in Lyons, France, on December 28, 1622. He had been traveling in the entourage of the king and queen of France at the time, but rather than stay in royal quarters, he lodged in the gardener's cottage on the grounds of the Visitation convent in that city. Fittingly for this apostle of the little virtues, he died in that modest cottage.

St. Francis de Sales was canonized in 1665. His feast day is celebrated on January 24.

Sophia Institute Press®

Sophia Institute

Sophia Institute is a nonprofit institution that seeks to nurture the spiritual, moral, and cultural life of souls and to spread the Gospel of Christ in conformity with the authentic teachings of the Roman Catholic Church.

Sophia Institute Press fulfills this mission by offering translations, reprints, and new publications that afford readers a rich source of the enduring wisdom of mankind.

Sophia Institute also operates two popular online Catholic resources: CrisisMagazine.com and CatholicExchange.com.

Crisis Magazine provides insightful cultural analysis that arms readers with the arguments necessary for navigating the ideological and theological minefields of the day. *Catholic Exchange* provides world news from a Catholic perspective as well as daily devotionals and articles that will help you to grow in holiness and live a life consistent with the teachings of the Church.

In 2013, Sophia Institute launched Sophia Institute for Teachers to renew and rebuild Catholic culture through service to Catholic education. With the goal of nurturing the spiritual, moral, and cultural life of souls, and an abiding respect for the role and work of teachers, we strive to provide materials and programs that are at once enlightening to the mind and ennobling to the heart; faithful and complete, as well as useful and practical.

Sophia Institute gratefully recognizes the Solidarity Association for preserving and encouraging the growth of our apostolate over the course of many years. Without their generous and timely support, this book would not be in your hands.

www.SophiaInstitute.com
www.CatholicExchange.com
www.CrisisMagazine.com
www.SophiaInstituteforTeachers.org

Sophia Institute Press® is a registered trademark of Sophia Institute.
Sophia Institute is a tax-exempt institution as defined by the Internal Revenue Code, Section 501(c)(3). Tax I.D. 22-2548708.